NOT EVEN THEN

The publisher gratefully acknowledges the generous contribution to this book provided by the General Endowment Fund of the University of California Press Associates.

NEW CALIFORNIA POETRY

Edited by	Robert Hass
	Calvin Bedient
	Brenda Hillman

BRIAN BLANCHFIELD

UNIVERSITY OF CALIFORNIA PRESS

Berkeley   Los Angeles   London

NOT
EVEN
THEN

poems

University of California Press
Berkeley and Los Angeles, California

University of California Press, Ltd.
London, England

Library of Congress Cataloging-in-Publication Data

Blanchfield, Brian, 1973–
   Not even then : poems / Brian Blanchfield.
      p.   cm. — (New California Poetry ; 11)
   Includes bibliographical references.
   ISBN 0-520-24038-3 (alk. paper)
   ISBN 0-520-24039-1 (pbk. : alk. paper)
   I. Title.   II. Series.

PS3602.L37 N67   2004
811'.6—dc22   2003015901

Manufactured in Canada

13 12 11 10 09 08 07 06 05 04

10 9 8 7 6 5 4 3 2 1

The paper used in this publication meets the minimum
requirements of ANSI/NISO Z39.48–1992 (R 1997) (*Permanence
of Paper*).

CONTENTS

KILL DEVIL HILLS

NOT EVEN THEN

ONE FIRST TRY AND THEN ANOTHER

Careful, a night set on edge
the European tradition of virtuoso
and the raw desire to articulate.
I pushed them both backward on the bed in the end
and each played on, one first
try and then another.
Soft then on succession thought.

The instrument all torso is loved where are held
fitting the flown down housemartin with a reed
or belying midway uncertainty
in tandem the hands, and acts adolescent.
A natural vaults a natural
development, his farther back barn jacket
American and strewn as if spare.

Thought soft the crescendo all along
saws, neither stroke inward or from the heart
except it begins unbecoming
building in roomy youth.
We have our no, libido, go.
Then all limbs arms and loudly I don't want to
play down the skillless touch.

WEREMEN

THIRTEEN POINT THREE THREE

A cunning policy, the sunrise
announcing new and same with light,
its body east, shot as it was stalled
late west and, to broiling score, identifiably.
We knew there had come a night and gone.
We knew Cujo was under the engine,
as ever, as three into ten goes three, fucked
by dog on chance of sound in shade,
by sun on car far, God, from help.
All the while in the world,
empathy subsists on estimation.

Having, during any second, human
disbelief in perseverance to outrun,
thirteen and a third shots, stills as it were,
are needed to make what isn't real. Or more, per.
The museum of the moving image is dark.
The medium is dark, dark as a decimal.

Numbers on residential Queens facades
rise or fall by twos indefatigably.
It scares me from the museum how far I go walking.

How do we go in the dark?
We come home, commonly. If we can't cover it
with retained image more rapidly than
a thousand times a minute, the flick discovers us.

The movie says A you A_1 you A_2 you A_3.
Host and hostage stir. We wish, to see.

Take away interruption and continuity
has no brink. Icemen dazzle as sons date.
Let's go over interruption once more.

Continuity, but a policy through the boroughs
(how many stops between time and $time_2$?)
is insistence there be a train, like Cornell's el,
by bridge hoists and windows breaking light,
idling into the shock, yours, of a silhouette repairing.

The medium has one, me,
two, not minding going for it.

The car door cracks before it opens wide. It wavers,
catching dementia's attention,
like a needle at the bottom of a pool.
Any dream we have is a far film come to this.
The eye, for a lapse a hilt of sword,
scans as anon what looms.

LETTER TO A SILVERY MIME IN YELLOW

I knew you'd not adjust the tug on principle. Even so
the reason I first sat and return where it's dirty is sexual.
I cannot disabuse myself of motivation as an acorn might
its casing. Then it helps you stand so straight in your postulate.
Then the world and Union Square station are painted on, if
just you. There are visits in a visit that have to do successively
with the stay. I was wearing these pants in my last
letter I think. If there's a better boy way into metaphysics,

again may I say yours is perfectly pulled across.

The sunniness signs on you somewhat more than silver did,
but these passers through carry pantries of selves along, miss
the pouring parasol, and think advertisements about you.
Sell me nothing of your stillness stock so I can say so, even
poorly. I recognize my copy chief and dare her to look at us
when she throws me one and turns it old as cola on the floor.
A way to stay to regulate. Chance is in the long run concentrative
you mean? I am not a shade the same as you. I am late.

You are like Kant's dove, winging a vacuum, even inching not.

When I was fifteen in the public library I'd find in greater
metropolitan phonebooks other Brians' addresses
and write away to them for help, Brian, dear on principle.

Sometimes when I'm too much in the waves of us you wash
in, I'll find myself outside italicizing a wire of birds

with an imaginary cursor. Or I am the cursor, and
the wave won't take over. Do you anticipate the drop of this
before you? Our trembling hangs on so twisted a stem; even so,

the six train runs beneath us and stacks the two bills
in your foot locker, leveling an all along crisp dispute.

FERDINAND, THE PRIZE

It then emerges that the interpellation of individuals as subjects pre-supposes the existence of a Unique and central Other Subject, in whose Name individuals [are interpellated] as subjects . . . "And the Lord cried to Moses, 'Moses!' "

LOUIS ALTHUSSER

bull whose sperm goes for two hundred dollars an ounce,
phantom father and jerked god of Vermont, the likes of whom
are yet unknown, Ferdinand folds in his forelegs and huffs.
How many my size he equals! How few of us here I am!
The visit in a machine must have its sanctity somewhere

in its mastery. Admit this siring business becomes confusing chore
after the first few promising lessons. What do you say, champ?
A hum, common to industrial dough kneaders, to each high
motorized rump, is easily reproduced in a mindless task.
The hum in humans turns televisions on. And then, depression
by a sudden outage. Him whom? The afterthought is, if not hurt,
slowed by imminence, a live wire pulling along this fence to shrink us.

How does he meet with this largess(e)?
Were it an advance
in evolution to dream on demand less bovine contractions,
I'd not think it bold of selection to carry this candidate.

The shock of blonde hair, though, strikes at who's the bull's god,
at whose is each shock's private pull at Ferdinand. If you can believe,
There are no subjects except by and for their subjection.

And Ferdinand answering, yes, it is really I, Ferdinand,
but beastly, at some level freely coming to the reservoir, the maker

met. Coming so far, always-already Ferdinand, to a so-be-it.

——————

It seems smaller and less just, what I said, not *amen*,
said for entertainment, really, hearing that it got back to you:
the inconceivability of our ever having been together rivals
the mechanical bull or some such remote craze. Look at me, love.
Nor do I mean each night to hail you, but name you anyway
a blacked exactness I can manage, a shift toward me and,

were it an advance,

a touch on my shorts after
                such strong candidacy.
How much like us visiting the sanctum, in the mats somewhere,
an earring, a blonde hair. There is no jolt
from experimentation, except in and through the experiment:

        the free hand a high phantom,
lost places something steer-thrown should have landed.

RED HABITS

Shame is my sister. She'll get no niece.
Agree in me a tenancy of junction and
a process of elimination. One has promises
and room for whom to keep herself.

A pinkening vibe, as from exit light in other halls,
mother-runs this cloister of disavowal,
and in the sobbed-inside cells locked to mine
I imagine the interferences explained

in don't-think-twice and reverse advice
and by habits for both head and breast,
hers and hers as red as mine at chamber check.
We are each herself a further interference.

At the hearing of the struck erratum,
the selfsame half convenes, claiming
men must have an obverse drill
and reading brother officers' reports:

Still we wait outside, our hooves shoed
improperly for the slalom ahead, or,
Today the drop died trying
to lock our icicles together.

THE WEREMEN

When Mister Ya
cried in my hands
great tears as new as mine,
but like a doll's, in Chinese
I said I am scared too.
Joseph Rock, the botanist,
who made Lijiang his base
for expeditions in 1922,
a magazine's man in China,
who for twelve years
hired four *coolies* a day
to carry his makeshift divan,
who wrote it off
and sent the Smithsonian
thousands of specimens of
shrubs and even orioles,
which mean love, who dressed
in white, which meant death,
always, and had personally
seen blue sheep in Tibet,
had personally taught
him his first English.
My name translates into a word
that means blue, but
it's only phonetic.
By virtue of his brushwork
and knowledge of the classics,
Teacher Ya headmastered

the village's school
and lost fourteen years
of prison's worth of mind.
In ten days, I could not freely
remember why I was not
whom he was sure of.
He showed me Rock's old pliers
and started me on two primers
of the Na Xi dialect, inscribed
to Student Blue. In earnest,
lessons into the chirping night
kept me. Like Zhuang zi, was I
one butterfly's worth of man.
I remember I had a shameful
wet dream in the cinderblock
hostel about lying about
pressing against a wall others
peed on, and stomach pains.
Then, earlier always
than I, was Ya at the door
with magnesium tea and
instructions for going
up a mountain,
where, at what possible time
of day! only the underbellies
of leaves were lit in an ardor
every green begins to mean,
and for coming down to find him
who shone at the bottom,
whose elbow I learned to hold
through town a pace behind,

whose students' children gave us
persimmons they had grown
for his moving past, but whispered,
whose white moons in water
under branches on rice paper
were political in ways
I do not feel as Chinese
feel. Anew, his tears. And in those
full, occluded moons
I struggled personally to find
the sky under which I
was a white man waving,
which meant leaving him,
unconvinced of the end,
even of the poem I'd not slept
to write against the hostel desk.
It scared me to teach it.
I was as old as he was
when Rock left to die—far off,
at home. With gardens in his name.

The moon will all but disappear, which is to say the world is in the way again. It will take two hours to return to full, which is what we, in our way, call a whole half lit.

The last eclipse I didn't understand what I do now.

I was stunned by lawn sculptures of waves outside the long lobbied Delano on South Beach, its oceanside wide open, its twenty-five-foot billowing white drapes sucked to my back and then not and then sucked again, its cavity fighting mine.

The galaxy is all wrong with a nine-dollar cosmopolitan. I couldn't get daylight's alibi. Someone said gimme an O. I said gimme another. We couldn't get the bartender's attention. Obtundity nearly knocked me over.

Dennis said he didn't know about lunar ones but the wind that rushes in when the sun goes out brings the scent of your secret desire.

At Grand Army Plaza, by nine lanes spinning into fewer, I make it to the middle. The moon is already phased to the size of an eyelash, or someone's distant hand cupped at his sunned brow, making you out. Poor white parenthesis, is everything inessential? Should everything come between? Someone cheer the sidereal.

But no one has outsprinted our coverlet to star in a warmth on rock. I imagine it new, another tournament beginning, an open, an invitational.

BORROWING A PAGE FROM NATURE

I wanted to know more about you; I checked out a book
on high-dwelling caterpillars in the Hudson River basin area,
figuring, start small, cover a territory, but the creeps
amounted to burn marks on your verandah
where you sometimes expire too tired to ash. I stay awake, trying to
see what instead is moving.

The rim of your pail has made permanent marks on
the backs of your arms. Cross them and there's a kind of corsage.

Those days at home I practiced mixing more remover,
my life took on meaning's warning.
It wasn't rock bottom, washing the sun off the roof in the sun,
the green from the grass. Put a better map to the ground than that.
Our worksong was about how
you can't have what you've wanted forever forever ever. Or
keep what's got by means of means, by any means, et cetera.

To lengths, I learned about going. I thought about leaving.

There is at least one exemplary commensalism in nature,
involving the mongoose, but its associate escapes me
and duly the reciprocity. Does it ride around on a razorback?

To the cabin where we would find our ideal lovers asleep.
You come out hours later. Here they were

sleeping together all along. Wouldn't any sort of prince break & en
A test to collect their firewood and go along.
To the village. A slight return, a rosebed bypass.

It was some time before I knew we spoke the same language.
Every stroke a mulligan, a do-over. What is it you
said between sneezes launching butterflies? A month of Sundays
is a bad guess for a good long while. Mothers' days.

Police down in the boxwoods. At the railing, Tripitaka turns
to Monkey: Monkey make it last. Moreover,
spit in one hand, wish in the other. Come on, shake.

It's rascalry to sit still in the pie safe
with the secret and devise a look asleep
perforce to dream of
Romulus and Master Lambton
and spoil yourself. Rascalry but nothing worse.

I was passing forward another mint as we pulled out
of the Citgo when the buzzard flew
into the backseat of the LeBaron,
beat its wings unevenly and escaped, its raw head harmed.
Mother stopped again farther up because I had peed.

Forty-two words are legible from the observation deck
of the Empire State Building on a day this usual. "Undies"
is one you wouldn't imagine, and "you" is the last
alphabetically. The foggiest is "domino"
but chances are its aspect doesn't read.

IF THE BLANK OUTCOME IN DOMINOES
ADDS A SEVENTH SIDE TO DICE

A system builds around refusal of a system. Adrift
in flagless sabotage, ahead the fleet prolepsis in arrears.
I went with luck and I went without and to go is to give
a leave. My dowry is narrow as a strait, as collapsed and
goodness gushing a get up more sophisticated. One day, a tile
in the driven sand, the next like nothing else. Not in thirteen
new ways to play can the one that's wild be reconciled.

I send away for nothing. I let prepare the least and blackest bed
occasion, its foot its head and windowswidth its length,
and lay along a want of stars a piracy's bit of balance,
at sixes and sevens with facing's nature, the cross with danger
purity, and in the time it takes a stretch of beach to dry
and on a day when all the mail from Normal'd come,
in death's detail, both in its clutches and in its throes,
I make in love my ribs fit his.

Like the mention of a cousin or human touch,
you'll go months without the sight of blood
and then pass a payphone gobbed with it,
one for months you'll think never to use,
then ride the train with an immigrant balancing
a pool of it on his hand like a coffee lid
and see a dog draping a divider, emptied carafes,
and wake from a lively nap to know for hours
you have spurted it from a peeled, fretful cuticle,
to just miss a call from your best friend who
speaks of the quiet for a half hour at the bottom
of a flight of stairs at work she fell she kept,
badly bruised. She sang on the spot, she says,
about loneliness, and the quarter that spilled
from her she called you with. You listen.
It is kind of a throb under water to start
you going. There is a standard in it.

CHERCHER

first be lost in fatal tides

The world's new water route junks a mudded follower,
and a manor lands a bench, its back a high parapet
to alone look over over the settlement of one.
As though it were there forever, a woman slides in, sits
and digs through her sweats. By floodland she's meant
to live on fault's opposite; she dials to get her son on
the other end.
             Barbarianism is a mistransmission.
The lovers stood at the Canadian border and made believe
the no fly zone and flew paper planes with messages
side by side in French to whomever else lived
at one another's feet, a test of jurisdiction.

What is dear in dearness? I didn't sleep on either watch,
while yours was kept I thought to disappear,
on mine I really looked.

—————

On the Isle of Pines, Crane began *Eternity* with a trace saying
Barbadians had where storms blew clear through to aphorism.
His hurricane had speared the grove with exclamation marks.
Distancing, Winters answered favor was all withdrawn.

Nothing is unsearchable. There, the first word ever meant.
Salt allegiant to the sea collects however anywhere
it washes away. Sunbeats on the waves bespeak
barbarian adages for thunderstrickenness.
Then the compound is conceivable,

                                        the problem compounded,
balancing sign and again sign, though the moon may have turned
where I am lui-même. Take everything off yourself, let her
let him. A trove, stations beneath the heart. Recover.
Where do you keep your singlest secret Hotel Américain?

If a thing washes up it is refuse, but what of a seat,
which is a place or stop, a suggestion run firm. Its yield
and issue is indication no less than lowered from on high.
Rest is what a mother can do if she gets it.
By landmark she means an unsound standing by.

                                        She holds at it.

          ─────────────

Mont Royal is a park in Montreal. Imagine
not making it there. In a city by a bay you can say this
kiss has happened before. The Saint Lawrence is swift,
and, beyond the guard you near in my arms, swift refuse
nearer never. Protest relies on repetition.
Suppose the nurses

                        suppose the nurses'
aides strike-sympathetic. In an emergency abiding
mixed messages, or asked how a last press might feel,

anyone would turn mandarin on the easternmost reef of his cot,
catechizing the courtesan waters enceinte, careful
to touch not even himself until the end and then where.

Between two addresses, trouble has an origin,
the last one would see of the postman, jeep in the creek.
SEPTEMBER, REMEMBER! OCTOBER, ALL OVER.
What matters is the vacancy, draw comfort.
Visitors who tread the route here, poor patient
followers, find only the room lovers—whole bodies
sworn in by wind in the window bay—ever occupy.

To be honest, he lets me know when Venus is visible.
I receive them when she writes the water letters, burned.
There, at the top, floating.

Last night at the plaza, the NYC Correction van (a crime
when we have only guesses)
first whistled around and then drove slowly, illegally by,
radially in the traffic circle. I had been reading
from the Selected Burned Letters of the Author.

I had been swimming at the Y. The blurb from X,
I wouldn't bother, is what drew me. What *was* I thinking?

The back of the right hunch is a cage. It is expected
you won't want to go along. I had half a mind
to ask what seems the officer what seems the problem.
Some hope I dashed and some I asked back.

And so not friends exactly in Atlanta.
I sent him sentiment's distance and parts of Barthes.
Swimming no less than perpetuated falling convinces me
even bearings' errors are bearings. On the plaza steps
a moistening begins to move me. We packed a U-Haul
that rode me like a *n'est ce pas* on the ramps.

The driver parked and whistled to himself. I was thinking
—in his words *If I were you*—about night.
With farther ardor, the van chirped, a reverse patrol.

It being a plaza, there was in every wet leaf a public
document. The pigeons were self-sunk like hand puppets
in the Clenched Fist Repertory. There was one reply:
a brown page begs the ground the same question,
the blank facts face down,
not to be addressed until the opposite happens.

ISLAND EQUIDISTANT

THE SAME QUESTION

Weissmuller lifts himself out second.
A pool is a somehow still part of a stream.
Send in a hat of pith close to current;
it fusses at distinction and keeps a winding oath.
The two had toggled at the bank, to a watery
reprise; there's another trick in the scene ashore.
They sit in confrontation, folded thrillingly
at the meridian of first facing. He prepares
a lesson on sight and reaches to hide her eyes
when Jane has the better idea, giddy atop
the promise of sex with a swimmer, to mirror
her hand against his,
then disoblige the likeness applied,
turning it, as the sound to the sea,
measure for countermeasure
"different. Do you like the difference?"

Where have I been, so new to nature?
I helped the drifter you sent to my rock bed;
there now. He says it's the same body,
water the one world over.
We shifted stones in the brook and asked
one another the same questions about you,
and troubled the water masterlessly.
Turned us right up onto a public beach. You should see
the calcified tail he found in a Snapple bottle.
We fed lines through the terrarium at the aquarium,

fogging the wall about the thirsty darlings: *How*
everything cascades all over again, and *why,*
whom have I crept alongside, somehow still,
piloting the world over my one life
on elbows to, at the least level, drain
my recalcitrant head in his hand and some sand.

PROPELLER OR CHIME

Mobile, the elements could but do not touch.
Even if they wanted to? This, passing,
the passing looking like lying along
a tail that coils and volunteers a beat,
is to a tomatillo an osage's moon. You cook it
out of love. It's dressed in overcompensation.
I watch your disappointment and suspect
you're sexy, but drill myself on moving right
by. There's no handle on this. Passing
for inattentive, inattention pulling
as at sutures till they weep, a trickle
escaping, enjoining even wanting to
—surprise surprise two estimation marks—
step rung from sleep's low rung awake.

Imagine things in sympathy have somewhere touched
or not yet. The episode originary motivates their likeness.
I'll thread anything through this light. Eventual, never
by bewailing the eventual—flickering—an impetuous
deathwish gathers footage a length of sentences premature
to say. Wind in ivy and estrus terror qualify, text

translucent. Not yet this morning I was sifting subtext,
apprised by radio all originary night, a night a touch
I fear unfinished, of contingencies' premature
helicopters. Patrolling outside phenomena for likeness,
sleep read a sound trailing off and, impetuous,
returning as essentially the walk my house to yours. Never

now unparallel, trouble covers its own shadow whenever
aboveboard. Lift off and devastate, this is only a test.
I'll thread anything through this light, impetuous
heterogeneity in the sundown beam. We were touched
to have sussed a moment's true content, or the likeness
anyway. Touching disappointment, to bear its imprimatur.

I have a soft spot, and if I may, I take it back, the premature
renunciation. I do want to die in my underwear, in ever
diminishing returns your house to mine. An outward likeness,
that is, different on the way back, motivated by the pretext,
originary news, that all is exercised by terror. It touched
off a spate, a spree, a bulletin dalliance of impetuous

eventualities. Mock emergency rattles the impetuous
alarmists. Worry, if to lead with disregard or, premature,
to follow is scant advantage. Seattle stands. A touch
aboveboard, trailing off, a pass. The only enzyme never
stuck for words is replicase. It writes the sticky text
it reads. It parts a sympathy and leaves a likeness.

Figure sewn aground, sky broken open, and likeness
bid goodnight. Good morning, fungibility. Impetuous,
I froze a hailstone for you, itself above and below in text-
book agitation. In the other world, if it isn't premature
to speculate, it's called a cave pearl, or not yet. Never,
as it were, yet, we on land wave. Contingent on it, touched

somewhere we on land wave. In bed the Never architects
pull blueprints to their chins. Its patterns premature, impetuous
dream runs all night the house's likeness. It starts at any touch.

Not the one in the James A. Farley flagship
office, where neither gloom of night
should stay a courier from rounds appointed,
by whose oath Eighth Avenue is twenty-four
headstarted and bulbed blocks old,
cloven from Hudson at the simple tract
of Abington Square's triangular need
(where a grid doing up an obliging island
most struggles to keep a straight face),

nothing indeed for tellers to man, but
statistician speak for sampling
a populace of incidences in and over time.

Over a calendar, the window glances,
its block plot in search of concentrations
daily, and, order be framed, corners chance's
concessions to what will coincide.
By ways of example.
Here is a craft. The kind to ride,
a certain cursor modeled on unengineering.
Witness Dr. Dia with the journals of Jung
prove nothing had designed the mentions of fish,
darting in sixes at glass-bottomed science.

It is precarious, the hovering
purpose a tour of its deck throws over,

bedeviling a day that stayed you in Brooklyn,
in breeding addresses of idiocy's sons, cropping,
seminomaddening up.

Where it is afternoon, every truck below is empty.
How loudly nothing presses beds into terrain.
Where it is night, hate a cat in heat.

Hate its odds.

INFRACTION

The body hurries. And then not pants, after all,
is the trouble in the offing, the percent sign
with the little o's these legs went to wear.

Why have math wrecked by the bed? Is any
aptness outlasting the stereo's shuffle mode,
planted hours ago, tracking our hideous goodnight?

So fast a fit so singular, one warms to it, a pledge;
"the world never this complete" contracts
this morning. It came over me, nothing over nothing.

As far as possible. A rose, a hundredfold as hard.
Sick lift, rule, am I not enough divided? Quick, if
chancing any dismount chances shame.

Crotch high, the problem will not, itself a hundredth
the privation of pain, be pressed and hurry out.
I am the standing offer, steeped in claim, in terms.

Normally a hootowl, a little professor, a dolly
to roll away on its denominator, what was withheld
engorges me. It splits the place of symmetry

and holds the arms at disagreement, number
every heartbeat breath. It has me qualify. Not pants,
put where I meet, where bearing gets.

THE ENDOWMENT BECOMING LESS AN INSTITUTION

The Endowment for Long Mornings in Bed
would like to recognize your continued contributions to wonder,
     at large,
and, for the project outlined in your proposal to get two glasses
of ice water from the kitchen, is pleased to grant a day's residency
in warm covers. Generous Endowment. A stretch.

I see you have seen another room. Its freshening finishes.
The freezer is sad, come back.
The day we don't fail doesn't miss us.
Think of the best parts of *The Rainbow*.

I was thinking the honeymoon, the embryonic swim out of time.
But will one of us build a church on the premises and say, as you say,
For both of us? I see it is me. A highmindedness the world
would only ground. Some air. Yes, have some space.
I will not frame arches, say enter.
The water is perfect in its own way, and your pillow is my pillow.

Still quizzical as far as the stirrup admits,
my first fracture recast the doctor's
anamnesis. My mother took the storm door
off of its hinges to get to the bike that pinned me.

Harley Davidson had meant to patent
the potato potato potato bleats
of its idle behavior when the Japanese
found their way
to the simple crankshaft layout.
Is a property property in traffic court?
The papers had a field day
with the case's dragging on.

Freud hires a carriage, goes to his patient's,
a place he's been a hundred times or more,
but he's not a leg let down from the buggy
before he knows the walk is different.
The driver is reproached and Freud is wound
around two corners, down a parallel street
to the home of his host with the number of both.
This is a fact and fact leaves its ghost.

Freud on foot goes there for a reason.
He never stopped touching the ground.
As scenario, this is the hypothetical.
But here he is, Freud, well short of his block,
not mistaken. Indeed, this is an imposition.

I want to settle it now with America,
with the press. I know what it looked like,
the kickstand in clover, my curious
proximity, the ongoing anguish. I'm dropping
the charges. I still have my name. I lost his number.
My foot forgives my father's Suzuki.

BLANCH WHITEFACE TO FACE

*[Flashlight-ushered to your seat, closing night. Fade house music,
the* Eponymous *album. Curtain up.]*

THE ACT OF THE CASE
The tables had turned in the trial and Wilde
bade behavior lie in it. Made Douglas lower
into worry, representing himself, the theatre
presiding, a hundred-year appellate overture.

Heels at the apron's lip, see our pivotal youth.
Lord upstage, the subject you stood down
to be, having or behaving chosen, stood.

THE CASE OF THE ACT OF BLANCH
Admittedly. We ask questions if you stand it.
The floor'd never leave Whiteface's feet.
The braves would have completed the dance

and introduced herself as such, the act alone
in Spirits on the River, the act if anyone (white
offstage and late with it) presses play. Maestro?
Her name cancels some of its Sioux self out.

THE ACT OF BLANCH
She bent. Dinner banter over river rush dampers
no drum of her bobbing doing. She kneebent
shallowly. Symmetry wasn't even on her side.
Repeat: she'd only throw virility into relief.

Were it I, I'd dream of their risen red
nipples, bounding just wide of her, and rising fire,
but the dream takes all there is of Blanch.

THE COMMONWEALTH
Countersued, the undefamed signs a deed
to his modern name, occupational occupant.
The call of it so mildly phenomenal hearers

hear it heard. He might but he hasn't yet said
no. He's run under with a blush concoction.
Douglas, look overshoulder. My humiliation.
He dips as into its coma, our agreement.

COMEUPPANCE HAS HATCHES

The way agrarians
make terraces,
a mountain wrap
without the first rise,
you keep asking.
Samsara, the great
inoperative screw—
ravel means unravel.
When you find you
are running the same
run of soy,

I catch you pressing
the spacebar well
past error, an act
of silence, a string
of wrongs. You drive
a character so fast I
can't make it out, the
lowercase gong
to end all documents.
That's the spirit.

A prince is
by definition.
A definition settles.
All God's squirrels get
darker as you go north.
At a certain point, three

lines look astral.
One up two away—
root root root.
From the corner breathing
comes a guest going
home, zeroing in.

Your backyard had the canyon where the house had planned to settle.
Your stepfather was an officer set on Atari before mine dined
the mother in Paris.
My backyard had the hill that made mowing acrobatic.
I said whatever you want to do when the mother worked. You kept
your dad's name. The house blipped, three men dying at turns.
Your hands had a sped age condition the mother made better
and my teeth chipped off on the road named Providence.
Bloom where you're planted you repeated
whenever I got tackled
in the canyon.
The plan was to go shirtless mowing the hill in the sun. It upset a man
to mow the hill otherwise.

From whose house's crawlspace did we see the fiancé through lattice?
The mother said I am your best friend always remember. Hands wring
differently for everyone why?
The truck my dad left had parking blocks you used
as ramps. The hill was no place to land. The sun
made its crisscross on our legs beneath the house.
I settled for a new name and a V-neck
and whatever made better the mother
but felt around foundation that if
the houses blipped and the blocks blew off and the road bloomed a hinge

and folded over like a felt box closing
around a band,
the canyon
given the hill
would betray the condition of crawlspace

and fill the land.

Newfoundland gives Labrador its first ice report since June
each November. Labrador listens to radio Newfoundland,
more closely during daylight savings. A last vessel parts
a maritime province for the Atlantic, last though others after radio in
with cause. Dimensions then are time and gist that had been
constant distances. A young man dangling in his berth a foot or so
under water feels the viscid passage require a new course of him.
Oxygen, make red mean go again and blue come back.

There is nothing says two men on the three weeks new inch
can't tread the strait to a small, mountainous granite
island equidistant, two dogs lost though no one's there.
The zombie fog makes the lighthouse lean. Dawn reveals hair by hair
each asterisk in the glassy ground like second hands and Labrador
in light of Newfoundland, but almost at once. Off-color,
a good story about geese before, at once, the station fades.

The double A batteries popped from their bubble scrotum and flung
into terrain atop a roof are, as well they should be,
rolling either's groundswell into tandem gears.
Ribbon unto ribbon, on axes lateral under skies. In June
again nothing says go back in V formation.
The trail though is disappearing into theory, lest it bear repeating.

TO COME TRUE A THING MUST COME SECOND

Once was a story of following following.

Return is rarely the reverse I value or so I
led you like a zero out the zoo,
toured it twice at once from your regard,
and came to understand.

Roughing it, a captive is another whom
a captive asks, which one of us stays wilder.

We catch them polar in the Bronx
among the shots of me looked at in the eyes:
the check of one tactic—drowsing in the rear
but aware—against another—pacing the periphery.

ANSWER DAY

I guess there'd be no way I could say a heartbeat wasn't a pure move. But
ELIZABETH STREB

By that moment we crept onto the bridge and that moment remained
strung from tunnels one the parent dovetailing nicely and one put past us
each multiple into a several world. What if

I just retreat into the shade and you continue, talking taking in the sun.
Vanish and not once rehearse, leave tamped the grass uprearing near
your rhapsody, my goodbye at the bottom of a warm bowl only you fill,
only first a prompt. Alright what flavor ice cream does Olivier prefer?

Horizon collision is still no such thing awake at night.
Choreographer versus the single vantage. Is one standing
or is one left standing? Please embed
a franker engram.

When nothing to speak of sank,
then the Earth itself transcendent manifested a fold. But leave the tower.
The coming world too drags retrieval over the site I inmost lost you—
The listener you are the less alone.

Is nothing met in the black synesthetic? Must just be
a man has a vas deferens and, gradually,
two men have vas deferentia. Dovetailing is not a pure move.
A pure move is one which cannot be stopped.

I beat my heart back perpendicular. The ongoing will have its barrier
preeminent again and, to prove the course, again. Salvage may be lain
    like a bridge
on either side. Morning sets the vigil on end and raises even with
where were you the question of white buildings.

No rails for leaning over with the secret, though there she held.
The bed I am in is a feisty place it was allowed. Watch this.
Behavioral fix for nightmares: a sleeper practically has two sides.
Don't like what you see? It's built-in that you can alternate
—and then one hand forgot, a stroke of guarantee—
and the dream turns over too. I said which side of my face
is it unsafe on. No conjuring earlier or after this: it isn't fixed.
Why ugly doesn't last like that. Now and once I had a practice.
Now and once I practice having had a page no one in Winston-
Salem could ever read but me. Sleep behind me, against is good.
Leave my mother's other hand on you, should it close your eyes
so as to allow I cannot see what blessing I must half banish.

The night manager rounds the long motel.
Along the L of it, he leaves his youngly luck
in a plastic chair. They have a word, peut-être,
when he sits. The boy is made of discs, a stack
of plates one waiting for him may pull him in rinse with.

A beret to spin off, and off a fist, a head to uncalm.
But what is there—he names the number room we pull
apart and returns—*out there?* The night manager is not
without appeal. *More information* you ask as if to ask
Is this the end? You want me to identify.
Well, they are two sons of four and so on.
In the morning you are pulling apart

>   *Do you want to see something involuntary?*

and heading for the beach.
You are my truest friend is what I meant
or managed to betray by a stiff behavior.
I was wrong around an unfair question to be a boy again.

If I am wearing your nail polish, on two of ten occasions,
which wagerer's eyes are drawn amid a flush
on the dunes? An uncondition in two hands, this. Whether

>   *memorized? physical or something thoughtless?*

one has a choice you were sportive not to clarify.
Something supposed and young men's bodies have rules,
resist. Truest, honest is not a mock superlative for you.

Nothing's against one's will, here.
Only there is great determinacy going along with
Kill Devil Hills, North Carolina.
It was even sexy on the map, on the tongue, to the ear.
There was nothing in its set I would arrange. The appeal,
the poker game, the number room are the data of this science,
the food put to hunger. The rinse was mine.

Come lie on my towel . . . then, were I made to decline,
biding time alone, *not on my life*. It was midday.
I was burning. The tide, too, was returning, pulling.
It drew the sound of sound alone to register.

The science lasts, or it longs. Which is,
when left to chance, what

wakes one up the beach a bit, what recommends
the book he was reading, the fiction of a classicist
with a deep understanding of pornography, of the rule
of no rules ordering pairings within a set.
That one's as good as another to another is demeaning
of complexity, hands management its unease.

The one regular surge of you and the ocean sent
through me is like a dream, it occurred to me.
Van Gogh on his own took camphor for it.
A chance association. A full day on the surging coast
and longing make tours of a distance. Two of the same.

KILL DEVIL HILLS

When bird's markings replaced knotted cords,
writing first emerged.

LIU XIE (C. 465–522),
The Literary Mind and the
Carving of Dragons

Dyslexics unite, I mean, start over.

Play father at the switch doing his light on the subject routine
to make you mock upset about a kindred intrusion. To prate
to be invited in. Maybe you want to strain your eyes.

Here there's a map of the curling island in every room
on front street as if the strand were turned on self-similarity.
Back street runs along front street, flaring.

The single stream was still a luxury when in dollhouses adults
traded promises. We'll hang hand towels for our sexes and
at every faucet install an h and a c handle. Turn from without.
Not all longing is forward of her but put a window here at least.

It's untrue you can't release the instrument electrified.
Work mother at the faucet until you get the restorative pose.
Were a subjunctive little boy who'd develop his wink thingy
word for word. Or, spine in had she shelved his Just So Stories.

Of narrow technique, back street comes from behind so that
the last available turn is Ibound onto Thoubound.
Pilgrims who miss it line up lucy ricky out on the isthmus.

Flash lightning and wake swearing he was running water in
the dark to make her rush and switch the lights. Which

things are off in this room? Who, what, when, where,
and sometimes why need sons nonesuch as I apply?

He maketh me to come to a faucet, to come and turn off
Commercial, to read a map from without and quit promising

I have singlehandedly stopped the curling of American letters.

THERE ARE FIVE DEACONS

One of them drives a country cab, one of the injured ones.
Three of them are brothers. All of them are elders.
Two are widowers.

To begin with, you have four starmints left.
The woman next to you asks that you peel each before the sermon.
She is sister-in-law to the one with the tuning fork.

Two of them, one married, speak civilly to your mother even though
she is divorced. None of them has been divorced.
Two others, for good reason, have putrid breath.

You put a mint in your mouth when anyone speaks to you.

Two healthy deacons offer the hand of fellowship to their brother,
the brother who has led the song service (nobly, considering).

Your hand is candy red. The woman next to you
may not be allowed to know. The left hand
may not be the hand of fellowship. The naturally bald one
rejoins his wife from the far end of the pew, diverting her attention.

The one with the tracheotomy, whose wife answers *He's just fine*
when your mother asks, uses the electric belch only to say
a word to Preacher Newell at the end of each Sunday.

The good wife touches his gray hair and says he tells her you are
very special to his heart.
She means you two, when she says you.

The two with silver hair
have only hair in common except for being brethren.
One of them notes your mother's shortening bread.
You forget why this is funny but he gooses your knee each time
it's said. The other parks his truck down by the graveyard.

The sermon is about how the children of God
just know they are the children of God.
Preacher Newell explains it seven times and looks at you the eighth.

The one smoking a cigarette is waiting outside when you burst
from the church, folding
his wife's wheelchair into the van, asking if you are sick,
using the occasion to explain to you about the metal plate in his head.
He says don't you know if you're sick?

Can something be said here?
Who has a heart condition? Can you give his wife some sugar?
Why not?

STRING THEORY READYMADE

Number one, draw on your paper your paper on fire.
Get this down. Use this red. Any line you start
is a hose in half, and from third dimension
a fourth is siphoned, but that suggests as far as it goes.
By no power higher can you raise yourself and document.
Make fire, page one of one. With fire
or with red or with rise begin.

      International operator, come on with patience.
Once I have you I think that once I was imaginative
and more than once imaginary, closely
an ant at the date line climbing over.

I answered Susan Mensch's cell phone because it rang and,
from Four Seasons Chicago, Susan said she'd cancel usage,
so, darling, say hello in English remember I miss you.

If Duchamp made quite the New York snowshovel and from
scratch the vial of Paris air, such is art more material to love.
Once Mrs. Stephen Jay Gould makes a name for herself,
rest assured; everyone's units are like assholes, and there is one
theory of everything:

One's attention is not divided between following that car
and stepping on it. To have come by pursuit is fait accompli,

the skin and trail and look of getting out but not the serpent self.

RECEIPT

1° The Waterfall

See the source is farther
for relief, fainter undisturbed.
Sight is what we are within,
telling (day break) telling is
the light of it on current.
Here until next is which one
it is—a sin effect—keep it
keep it pinker than premier.

2° The Illuminating Glass

With rose as it were, *comme
comment dire*, arose rather two
flammabilities of art: one
a carbon copy of the first
ability to burn.

A WHOLE HOST

What there is as a surround to our figures

Reporting live from A Mountain
a branch is jammed high in a wash
and late by pairs the visitors aspire into view
beneath it and experience themselves commensurate,
stuck like something evidently thrust, then together
behave fallen unto, appointed, making gawky
gestures of ablution in the dry bed.
There I was no longer angry with my friend.
I wrote the words for given on his two feet
with bark and broke the skin, irresponsibly.

If all reproof in time meets with reproof,
we ask to return and redistribute papyrus among
the ephebes papering each his
carrel's narrow window or covering the word he
follows inaugurally each with another. We ask
to gain them admittance to the atrium, even
after sundown. Ought we, to ask, we ask.
There were many such passages in the complex,
lined with delegations of parity recombinant
with first-term Usage Panelists trading
or scoring passages in the orientation materials
they were asked to return unspoiled and
squandering their honoraria on bottled water.
We ask to restore contrast as the dial next to volume.
We ask to twist forgiveness into the desperation it is.

But already Act Three has begun.
Have ready the rope ladder for Juliet's nurse.
The dramaturge cannot overemphasize
the significance of its drop and retraction.

The copper averaging the burst brown glass aground
and, sudden and whole, the new nearness of the reeds:
night. At night alone, I saw with what above resolve
to cheat. Here there are no preparations to recount.
Given was someone cast consecutive eyes,
Appointed, a die drawn on, the lead waiting at the rail
to take my arm, her spellbound back to me like Beatrice.
Resolved, an artist grown allergic to paint, breaking
from any medium you like into platelet hives
just thinking of it.
                    Behind the genius complex, no
matter, was a zendo, irrupt in the field of no
verticality and no horizon. There being but one way ever,
gray wavering withal, to avenge the white wall
its impermissiveness.

At the corner of Speedway and Swan, reporting live.
A belling, a horning, a diluvial charivari.
A garland, mostly strung, unfastened yet, of apatite.
It may be coming around the mountain that she comes.
It may be my imagination for all I, new here, know.

To best resist contortion, collect the ladder by its rungs.
The way to the catwalk is through the wings.

LITTLENESS OF BEING

Whenever you say yes I think you haven't heard my question.
My apartment has kept something of an axiom. Closer to you
is closer to the door. No matter where I am's the very wellspring
of Prospect Place. Farther the broker me.
                                        Reveal the monitor,
let the lens train squarely on the monitor, switched of a sudden on
to offer on itself depths of assent, interiority from the better
still. With yes, you're gone or between my own idea to go.

Apology, from Greek for speech, without or beyond it.
Closer to the door, I'm a giant restoring to the eyehole chin deep
the rubber head of Spock
                                I, when thinking little, pinch into the kiss
his ears can be made to peck, contingent on mindlessness, and remove
because I thought you made the single knock your trademark.
Of the Paramount insignia on his neck until today I took no notice.
I'd come out if conditions changed. Knock now and again if not.

Action. Mania, monster to follow. A searchlight against our window above the block they closed off to shoot the Godzilla remake woke me. The neck of a crane was nuzzling the cathedral downstairs, an edit away from fantasy. Zoom at will. You were still asleep. More perfect than 1:1 is no scale. I thought about it again.

The day we met, my friend Bethesda's boyfriend explained—about having let his roommate Manhattan crawl in bed with him every night she'd been gone—what's even funnier than pretending to do it. And he actually laughed, she said, and cried. It is funny, in actuality. Like sitting, standing, walking, sleeping isn't it.

An actual secret takes time, and a here-on-out, hypnosis.

When we went down for Chinese, every doorway had soldiers under walkmen, doomed extras waiting to shoot the illusion again. What *is* not razing, scorching, swatting, lashing? What good is camouflage on Twenty-fifth Street?

And, does Tokyo come back from something like this? In the original, they had to recreate everything in miniature and fill the screen, steady the camera. Now in New York, you put the succubus in afterward. Action mania.

Tanks edge, troops scramble, live, aiming for its eyes, for platforms on the craning crane head, a storey above us. The commotion is incomplete, an engine of cries withheld. Not so, laughs.

There is a light trapped in my eyes, which doesn't go when I close them. I crouch over you to see you, to make sure of you. The director calls for Continuity to prepare a second take, a mayhem more the same. I am thinking about it again. I am doing it, this time on location. Pandemonium never sleeps. You cannot pretend.

VELMA

The sweatered, squat one, remember, with glasses,
iterater of the dog's doings, the dopehead's score,
swiped often, but sound and blinking by episode's
every end. What keeps a Velma from harm?
What does one any? Any mystery she bested Chris Burden,
drives his diesel still, motoring through Tehran in sunburst

kneehighs? Iconoclasm was the bubble syndication burst.
So keep a Velma in the Channel Islands, ice the glasses,
click and drag her from the screen to Gaza, say, for burden
of proof of Palestine. The right book, on that score,
is a trick lever the chosen shelve to engage harm
or exact replication. Let Velma bless as episodes

epidemics, famine; episodes
where her eyes go lensless—Shaggy, is that you?—burst
with crisis, prisms in chance's haunts. No harm is due harm,
cavalierly, dearly, she need not say, flooring ploy, glasses
readjusted. Who clues her in when no cartoon horror score
introduces the quarantine of the cab I am chambered in,

kissed but left with a Muhammad Ali, whose burden,
true, is self, self-evident. A villain has episodes
of wanting to be i.d.'d, before all others one whose core
corruption goes undetermined. The taxi is set to burst
in a wordsbreath: champ, Western blot. Empty glasses
endure a high timbre. The velum worn on beauty is silk harm,

and mouthing a curse still promises something. No harm
in a touch of affection for bearing the burden
to escort a ghost chance uptown, given glass's
steamed reaction to the closeness. Love, into episodes,
into times, eight innings counted out at home, is what burst.
What blood has ending brought to test in a settled score?

Pretend there is no instrument arrangement in this score.
Let Velma be photolicensed in doomslip vehicles so harm
can move only laterally like easier animation, let bursts
of background repeat as to imply a journey's burden.
My block too is unmistakable, the consequent episode
where an ungagged captive explains to a glint on the glasses

what score, if it weren't for you kids, he'd've made. The glasses
never burden such hindsight; errors untold live a lost episode.
She adds to the rue another heist burst in the manor of harm.

I would. Can I have a moment? Is there a condition
behind the one you've laid out? Does one come
away with an erogenous impression? Her eyes are
browner than I remember and I suspect there
am I betrayed. Is there any depth to which I won't
hesitate to wade? Do you, wave, take this seed
and drown its use, to sport and to promise till
memory serves you well? And do you well
take to consommé as any cure worth its salt?
In the taste, a liquefaction and a liquidation.
A jam frees, a winter thaws, as one hide
becomes another, as one torch borrowing another's
fire splits nothing. A hair please from each.
If a child would now take the aisle and grow.
These are his wrists, each brought round with child,
with single ringlets. He hides your bond.
Boy, have you predilections?

                              Sir, for predicaments.

LESS AND LESS THAT IS NOT A HOTEL ANYMORE

after Ou-yang Hsiu

In my kiosk for one, I, for one, water-
colored on the grounds for concern.
And everywhere I ever lived
pined on a cinderblock in pencil.
The rubbing may give you ideas.

The princess never felt it more, the underlying
in pursuit, lodged, a tiny drum in
coverage and coverage of coverage.
But is there a way not to bespeak terrain?
Have you slept on my vitamins?

Small brother pressing
his stinging face against one's harp:
this will have resonance.

Set out for the sage that home again
may as good a place as any be.

There is come in welcome.
Seeing in seeing off.
Ever and forever to turn around.

Into the ocean floor I dramamean.
The word of a name is only as news of it, heard
through sleep, cross distances like a gun's report. Namesake
to trauma: I dry the overhearing up.

                                    Butte to fjord:
a dive condition. I meant dream. Amen.

Wake has the makings of surface truth, the gone along
sign. I took the ribbon end under, worshipful
of its way above me, to teach myself mutual, suspend,
and you followed with the other by its lonesome,
loving length to depth.

My mother does not swim. Does not show up
in jeopardy by the loungechair, by the pool.
Important only to the composition is the identical
lean of loungechair and laptop
screen, the unlikely twin aquamarine of nonuse.
An idea of interior then all but proves a sliding glass.
Into the lit pool in the picture, it is snowing,
which, along with not using flash, creates the effect
of jeopardy in the steam's gray-going yellow.
Where in it has she from even pinks gone black?
In the ice-met warmth, in the huge matter of release
I used to show her how she was in water.
Still, to hold her breath takes her whole face,
a child misunderstanding the hide part of the game.

The fortress we keep to vision is immaterial. It isn't
that gamma warns too violet from the woods
or not enough. The woman shaken from the woman's color
says days answer days uncertainly. By herself she found God
on a window I have seen at an age I have been.
No one looking into the bright rise of vapor from the pool
from the loungechair suffers, where-
as to find vantage strains
one in light, going under dark's importances, the one
I face or shook. A glare on the glass would end
with me here and her unmirrored in effect.
I could never show her how she was in the window.
It never ceased deepening disappearance that
in the same life she was my mother she shone.

lived ninety years and died but eighteen
days from ninety-one. "Attend"
the last birthday party <u>here</u>. It was a cold
observatory a boy on the web named Riehl
imagined where dear Mr. Tombaugh
looked for planet X in the wishes
still posted this old anniversary.
There is quality science in supposition.
He warmed at exaggerated distances,
welcomed little real cottoning onto
his universal isolation.

*. . . Pluto fascinated me as a boy but as I grow I find myself
being drug away* [sic] *from my interest by my education.
Once again happy b-day and many blessings.*

Pollen where light picks it up is moved
like loose fur, the wind in a lariat
of reckless providence. Manifest, its mad
character trounces the parade one year,
the day another year the wrongheaded caved
into the breezeway, demanding calming down.

The discovery of a twenty-four-year-old
dressing, bending forward, shooting up,
is not the 1930 one, not the same way genitive.
The body systems had complicated
the simple slump, the first emotions.
Autumn no sooner regrets to rain.

Dear Elizabeth Streb,

Congratulations on the MacArthur. You once said
something I espouse; it had me dating the dancer standing
on the sugared glass of your split second piece *Breakthrough*,
beginning the Q & A immediately. The same for desire, I find.
That you'd not give gravity up—it's how you show difference.
Anyway, you deserve it. And say hello to so and so.

At the first listlessness, detail.
It's Appendix A of everything human,
the reach around for what concerns him
and doesn't belong. An archer beginner
detaches his thumb. They illustrate it
in *Microsurgery*, the four things he feels.

Flexion: Stamp your thumbprint to your palm.
                    There now, four, once more.
Abduction: Gunpoint, half a field goal.
Opposition: Everything's okay, or the world's
                    smallest violin playing for you.
Grip: Hold the bottle steady, indian burn.

Dear Pluto,

Hi again. Forest Theatre, 1991. You'll recall how I am
made as much of each shadow that passes over me as I am
of blood and bone, farthest from mind in your manner of mass.
I am no longer given to episodes of perfect bearing having.
Please tell again the wealth of the Earth. Thanks in advance.

About nothing can you say the opposite
is true in zero gravity. Nock. Release.
Some advice. Three times NASA
lets the Streb company fall a distance,
a minute and a quarter total. A dancer
can only remember feeling lucky.

Dear Dr. C. Victor Jongeneel,
     Happy Thanksgiving. It has been close to impossible
to reach you, specialized in the remote field of avulsion
and preserve. Here, I have iced my challenger. I find
I have been drawn away from my concern by my belonging.
Many blessings last. Small doctor, correct me if I'm wrong.

THE LIVING MANY GO DOWN ONE

It is at the price of degradation that the mummified One turns into the living Many.

And with intentions.

She wants damage done. She wants to spin tops.
She wants one way to land all the way around.
From absolutes she spasms into skin.
She wants its healing, having hurt.

Fine. We said beauty should have to do with us.
There, is she cutting through our yard,
furious with little bees all come to life?

We catch her as a prism gets light to separate.
On the face of it an accident.
We let her in downstairs. We shall not touch her.
It has been our creed that an accident can be a little proof.
So common a thing is rarefied now. A frontier
summed, it ranges the day.

The night to her is nothing new.
Her breath is like nests in it.
It shall be her breath by the candle guttering
into its shadow, its miscreant odes in shadow
to the fall without ideal. In the night, life can live.
In the dark we take something from our pockets.

On the face of it, nothing new.
There were none more deserving of it
nor is one here who can keep it singular.
Something exposed in us wishes it were rock,
though the point of it is chandelier.

SOME NOTES

"One First Try and Then Another" is informed by the video work of Martin Schwember, which was used in the Ballett Frankfurt's production *Kammer/Kammer*, a work its director, William Forsythe, describes as "oriented around the idea of voice, instrumental and literary, that dilates between an immediate, raw desire to articulate and the European tradition of virtuoso."

"Thirteen Point Three Three": Reference is made to Joseph Cornell's short film *Gnir Rednow*, which reuses footage from Stan Brakhage's *Wonder Ring*.

"Letter to a Silvery Mime in Yellow": Charles Peirce, in an 1885 review of Josiah Royce's *Religious Aspect of Philosophy*, criticized Royce's brand of scepticism: "Like Kant's dove, you have been winging a vacuum, without remarking that you never advanced an inch."

"Borrowing a Page from Nature" is for Robert E. Moore.

I owe to Dan Partridge the titles of "From the Selected Burned Letters" and "Less and Less That Is Not a Hotel Anymore." The latter is informed by "Kiosk of Pied Spring," a poem by Ou-yang Hsiu, an eleventh-century Chinese poet. Thanks to Jerome P. Seaton.

"Code Orange under Love, Part I" is informed by the discussion in William Egginton's *How the World Became a Stage* of similitude and contagion as concepts integral to medieval "sympathetic magic." Apparently unrelated, a placard in the Sonora Desert Museum World of Darkness reads "Agitation produces both hailstones and cave pearls."

Equidistant from "Newfoundland and Labrador" is the granite island Belle Isle.

"To Come True a Thing Must Come Second": The title is the last stanza—without her line breaks—of Rae Armantrout's poem "The Creation."

"Answer Day" borrows the phrases "but leave the tower" and "white buildings answer day" from Hart Crane's "Recitative."

"Receipt" fits on a receipt for admission to the Philadelphia Museum of Art.

"A Whole Host": The opening phrase is from W. H. Auden's "Pleasure Island."

"Littleness of Being" is for Douglas A. Martin. "The Matter, with Abjection" is a tribute to, and a misappropriation of, his statement of poetics in the journal *Narrativity:* "My abjection was becoming the matter with my subjectivity."

In "The Discoverer of Pluto" reference is made to astronomer Clyde Tombaugh (1906–1997), since whose death scientists have demoted Pluto, his discovery, from planet to astral body.

"The Living Many Go Down One": The epigraph attributable to Michel Leiris is part of a passage—about misfortune as an element essential to beauty—quoted without citation in *Francis Bacon*, by John Russell, who writes that Bacon "at once" and "with a thick, flat nib" circled the passage in his copy of the unidentified "little book by Leiris" given to him in the mid 1960s. "Fact leaves its ghost," quoted in "Not of the Heritage Softtail Series," was a favorite saying of Bacon's.

ACKNOWLEDGMENTS

Grateful acknowledgment is made to the editors of the following journals, in which versions of these poems first appeared: *AGNI: "Chercher"; Barrow Street:* "From the Selected Burned Letters"; *Bellingham Review:* "The Weremen"; *Fence:* "Ferdinand, the Prize"; *Fort Necessity:* "The Next Landing," "The Endowment Becoming Less an Institution," "There Are Five Deacons"; *Green Mountains Review:* "The Discoverer of Pluto," "Photograph of without Reference to"; *LIT:* "Borrowing a Page from Nature," "The Living Many Go Down One"; *The Literary Review:* "Two Moons," "String Theory Readymade," "Receipt"; *Ploughshares:* "To Come True a Thing Must Come Second," "Red Habits," "Less and Less That Is Not a Hotel Anymore"; *Seneca Review:* "If the Blank Outcome in Dominoes Adds a Seventh Side to Dice"; *Slope:* "Infraction," "The Earliest Work of Literary Criticism," "Refinery," "Answer Day," "Newfoundland and Labrador"; *Swerve:* "Letter to a Silvery Mime in Yellow," "One First Try and Then Another," "Thirteen Point Three Three," "Comfort Proviso with Shadow"; and *VOLT:* "Even Funnier than Pretending to Do It Is Actually Doing It," "The Same Question," "Chances at Kill Devil Hills," "Pipe Dream of a Deputy Best Friend."

TEXT:	9.5/15.5 Janson
DISPLAY:	Interstate
DESIGNER:	Victoria Kuskowski
COMPOSITOR:	BookMatters, Berkeley
PRINTER AND BINDER:	Friesens Corporation